Geography Success

STARTER BOOK

Terry Jennings

OXFORD
UNIVERSITY PRESS

Acknowledgements

The author and publisher would like to thank the following for help in the preparation of this book:

Air France; Mr Clive Hazelgrove (Optician); Hawkhurst Church of England Primary School; Mull Tourist Office; Mr George W Campbell (Scottish Ambulance Service); Mr G E Ellis (Mull and West Highlands Railway Company Limited); Vision Aid Overseas (www.vao.org.uk); Sight Savers International (www.sightsavers.org.uk); The National Dairy Council; Manor County Primary School, Uckfield; Linda Trimby; Jeremy Cottam.

Photographic credits

Air France p 23; www.JohnBirdsall.co.uk. pp 19, 50 (top); Brighton and Hove Library p 36 (both); Mr G W Campbell p 33; C F Capen p 45; Corbis/Owen Franken p 24 /Dean Congers p 54(bottom); Corbis UK Ltd p 54 (top); James Davis pp18 (bottom), 40 (bottom), 41; Eye Ubiquitous/D Burrows p 18 (top) /R D Battersby p 20 (bottom) /Geoff Redmayne p 24 (top) /David Cummings p 37 /NASA p 52 /Leon Schadeberg p 57 /Julia Waterlow p 58 (bottom); Terry Jennings pp 13 (all), 26, 27, 28 (bottom), 30 (both), 31, 32 (bottom), 38 (top), 40 (bottom),44 (top), 51, 55, 58 (top); Milepost 92½ p 22 (bottom); Mull and Highland Railway Company Limited p 32 (top); National Dairy Council p 50 (bottom); Sight Savers International p 49; Skyscan/Nick Hanna pp 28 (top), 38 (bottom); www.tografox.com/R D Battersby pp 7, 20 (top), 21 (both), 22 (top, middle, left, right), 23 (bottom), 25, 29, 42, 46 (both), 47 /L R Miles pp 8, 9 /Claire Williams pp 56, 59; Vision Aid Overseas p 48 (both).

Cover photo: David Cumming: Eye Ubiquitous/Corbis

Maps (pp 26, 30, 53, 56, 60, 61) GEOATLAS © 1998, 1999 Graphi-Ogre

OXFORD
UNIVERSITY PRESS

Great Clarendon Street, Oxford OX2 6DP

Oxford University Press is a department of the University of Oxford. It furthers the University's objective of excellence in research, scholarship, and education by publishing worldwide in

Oxford New York

Auckland Bangkok Buenos Aires Cape Town Chennai Dar es Salaam Delhi Hong Kong Istanbul Karachi Kolkata Kuala Lumpur Madrid Melbourne Mexico City Mumbai Nairobi São Paulo Shanghai Taipei Tokyo Toronto

Oxford is a registered trade mark of Oxford University Press in the UK and certain other countries

© Terry Jennings 2001

The moral rights of the author have been asserted

Database right Oxford University Press (maker)

First published 2001

British Library Cataloguing in Publication Data

Data available

ISBN 0 19 833844 9

10 9 8 7 6 5

Editorial, design and picture research by Lodestone Publishing Limited, Uckfield, East Sussex www.lodestonepublishing.com

Illustrations by Kathy Baxendale, Kate Chitham, Peter Kent, Jon Riley, Martin Sanders, Graham Smith, Peter Visscher

Language and teaching consultants: Ann Mepham, Julia Ware, Donal McCarthy

Printed by Gráficas Estella, Spain

Contents

(and suggested order of teaching)

My classroom

Look at this picture of a classroom.
Is your classroom like this?
How is it the same?
How is it different?
How many children can you see in this classroom?
How many children are there in your classroom?

Sorting shapes

Look at the picture carefully.
How many things in the
picture are square?
How many things have a
rectangular shape?
How many things in the
picture are round?

sugar paper

felt

fabric scraps

white paper

Shapes in your classroom

Now look around your own classroom.
Make a list of the things that are round.
Make a list of things that are square or rectangular.
Make a list of shapes that are on the walls.

Activities

1	2	3	4
cup	tin of beans	shoe	chair

A	B	C	D

1 Look at the drawings in the top row. Match each of these things with the drawing of what it looks like seen from above.
(The drawings are mixed up.)

2 **a** Put some things on the floor. Look down at them. Draw what they look like.
  b Now imagine you are looking down on your classroom. Draw what your table and chair would look like. Draw the things that are on your table in their correct position.

My school

What is your school like?
Is it large or is it small?
Is it old or is it new?
What materials is it made of?

This is a picture of a school.
It is an old building.
What is it made of?

A plan of the school

What do you think this is?
It is a **plan** of part of the school in the picture at the top of the page.
It shows what the building looks like from above.

playing field

school

fence

school

playground

fence

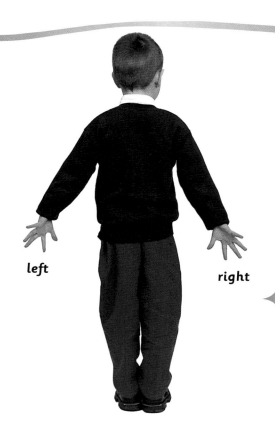

left   right

A plan, like a **map**, helps us to find our way about.

How would you get from your classroom to the playground? Draw a plan to show your route. Describe your route to a friend.

It helps to know which is your left and which is your right!

Activities

1 Look carefully at one side of your school.
  a Draw a picture of that side of the school. Draw
    ● all the windows
    ● all the doors
    ● all the drains and drainpipes.
  b What materials were used to build the side of your school?
    Label these materials on your picture.

2 a Write a sentence saying what you like about your school buildings.
  b What don't you like about the buildings?
  c What would you like to change?

You could record your ideas on a class tape.

The school grounds

The land around your school
building is called
the school grounds.
Some schools have only
a playground.
Other schools have gardens
and a playing field.

This picture shows part of the grounds of a school.
What can you see?
What time of year was it when the picture was taken?
How can you tell?

Your school grounds

With a group of friends, draw a plan of
your school and its grounds.
On your plan, draw and label tidy places.
Draw and label untidy places.
Where are your school grounds quiet?
Where are they noisy?
Mark these places on your plan as well.

Activities

1 a Draw a picture of your school playground.
  b Now draw another picture of your playground as you
    would like it to be.
  c What would you add?
  d What would you take away?

2 a Look at the plants in your school grounds. How many
    plants can you count?
  b Can you name any of them?
  c Find out what the plants need to live.
  d Who waters them and looks after them?

3 a Go for a walk around your school or school grounds.
    Draw your route map.
  b Show your map to a friend. Ask your friend to work out
    where you went.

My home

Where do you live?
If you live in the country, your home may be on its own or in a **village**.
If you live in a **town** or **city**, there may be many buildings around your home.

Different kinds of home

What is your home like?
There are many kinds of home.

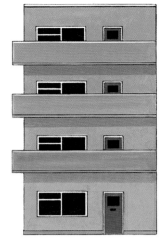

This is a block of flats.
Separate families live in each **flat**.

This is a detached house.

These houses are semi-detached.

These are terraced houses.
How many houses can you see here?

This is a **bungalow**.

Tom Thumb
Tiny Cottage
Small Street
Littlehampton
West Sussex
BN17 3AL

Your address

What is your address?
Everyone has an address.
It tells people where you live.

Make a card with your name
and address on it, like Tom
Thumb's. Draw a picture of
your home on your card.

Activities

1 Copy this chart.
   a Use your chart to record
      the number of different
      types of home that you
      see on a class walk or
      on your way to school.
   b Which type of home is
      most common?

home	how many?
detached	
semi-detached	
terraced	
bungalow	
flat	
other	

2 Choose one room in your home.
   a What do you and your family use that room for?
   b What things are there in the room?
   c Make a model of the room.

3 Work with a friend. Talk about why houses have numbers
   or names. Who needs to know?
   Tell your class.

My street

What is the **street** like where you live? How long ago was it built? If your area was built more than 100 years ago, the streets may be quite narrow. This is because there was less **traffic** then. There were no cars or lorries.

Newer roads

If you live in a newer area, the roads may be wider. The houses may have garages and driveways. There may be blocks of garages for the flats.

How many kinds of street furniture can you see in this picture?
What are they used for?

Buildings

Are the buildings in your street all the same?
What are they made of?
Can you tell if they have been changed over the years?

People used to get all their water from this pump.

People used this scraper to clean the mud off their shoes before they went indoors.

Horses used to drink from this trough.

Street furniture

Look at the picture of a street. As well as buildings, traffic and people, there are lots of other things in the street. These things are called **street furniture**. On the ground you may see covers and signs that show you where pipes, cables and drains run under the street.

These are all kinds of old street furniture.

Activities

1 Draw and label all the kinds of street furniture you see on your way to school or on a class walk.

2 a Draw a sketch map showing your route from home to school, or the route of a class walk.

b On your map, draw some of the important buildings you pass on the way.

3 Choose three of the buildings you see on your way to school or on a class walk. For each one, find out

a what materials were used to make the building

b if the building is old or quite new. How do you know?

Local jobs

What is a **job**?
Can you name some jobs?

Different groups of jobs

We can divide jobs into groups.

- There are people who make or grow things.
  Car workers and builders make things.

- There are people who take things from the land or sea.
  Miners take coal from the land.
  Fishermen take fish from the sea.

- There are people who sell things.
  Shopkeepers sell things.

- There are people who help us.
  Fire fighters and teachers help us.

car worker

builder

miner

supermarket check-out worker

teacher

worker on an oil rig

fisherman

office worker

**Look at these pictures of jobs.
Which group does each job belong to?
Try to think of more jobs for each group.**

police officer

factory worker

forestry worker

printer

train driver

Jobs and places

Some jobs can be done almost anywhere, such as being a police officer.
Every school has a caretaker or site manager.

Some jobs are found only in certain places.
Farmers work in the countryside.
Sailors work on ships at sea.

telephonist

market trader

Activities

1 Make a list of the jobs people do in your school. Find out what work they do when you are not at school.

2 Work in a group. Draw three large circles on a sheet of paper. Label one 'I make things'. Label the second circle 'I sell things'. Label the third circle 'I help people'. Collect pictures of the different jobs people do. Stick each picture in the correct circle.

3 Make a class chart of people who help us. Show the name of the job and what the people do.

My changing area

All places change. Some places change very slowly over many years. Other places change quickly.

Old and new

Look carefully at these two pictures. Can you see some changes?
What are they?
Think about:

- the roads

- the traffic

- the buildings

- the people

- the land.

Which of these changes do you think are good? Which are bad? Which of these towns would you like to live in?

Part of a town in 1900

The same town today

Finding out about long ago

Old photographs and old **maps** show us what places were like long ago.

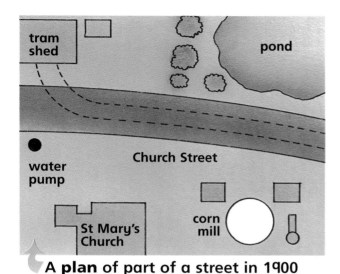

A **plan** of part of a street in 1900

Some street names give us a clue about things that used to be there.
'Castle Street' may mean there was once a castle nearby.
'Mill Road' may mean there was once a windmill or watermill nearby.

Activities

1 a Make a class display of old photographs or postcards of your area.
  b Try to find recent pictures of the same places. What changes can you see?

2 a Make a class list of street names in your area.
  b Are any streets named after things that are not there today?
  c Find out how other streets got their names.

3 Work in a group.
Do you have grown-up friends or relatives who have lived in your area for a long time?
Ask them how the area has changed since they were young.
Write down what you have found out.

Local traffic

Every day, cars, lorries and buses travel on our roads. Some roads have lots of traffic; other roads are quiet.

Traffic problems

Cars, lorries and buses can be noisy.
They make the air dirty.
Even when they are parked, they may block part of the road.
They make it dangerous for people to cross the road.

How is the traffic causing a problem in this town street?

Traffic is not allowed in all streets. People may walk in this street but they must not drive.

Controlling traffic

How can villages, towns and cities deal with their traffic?

Some places have a **bypass** around them. This keeps away traffic which is not visiting the place.

Some towns and cities have a 'park-and-ride' system. People leave their cars in a car park on the edge of the town or city. Buses then take the people into the middle of the town or city.

How does your village, town or city deal with traffic?

Have you used a park-and-ride bus like this?

Activities

How much traffic goes past your school? Make a traffic chart like this.

Start 11·00 Finish 11·30		Total
Cars	|||| |||| |||| |||| |||| ||	27
Lorries	|||| |||| |||	
Vans	|||| |||| |||| ||||		
Others	||||	

Put it on a clipboard. Stand outside the school gates if you can, but stay on the pavement near the school wall or fence.

Your teacher will show you how to record the traffic. Each time a car goes by, record it in the space marked 'cars'. Record every lorry, van, bus or motor bike.

a How many motor vehicles did you see?
b Which kind of vehicle did you see most?
c Do this survey again at a different time of day. Are your results the same?

Making my local area better

Look carefully at the area around your school or home. Where is it dangerous because of traffic? What could you do to make your local area safer? Here are some ideas.

Does your school have a fence like this to stop children running straight into the road?

Pavements

Is there a **pavement** outside your school or home? Who is allowed on the pavement?

The safest place to cross the road is where there is a 'lollipop' man or lady.

Do cars and other **vehicles** park on the pavement? Is this dangerous? Why? Do people ride bicycles on the pavement? Is this dangerous? Why?

No parking!

Are there any places where cars cannot park? Parked cars stop you seeing clearly whether the road is safe to cross, or not.

Street lights

Street lights make it easier for you to see and be seen at night and in bad **weather**.

Pedestrian crossings

Look at this picture. It shows a **pedestrian** crossing.
Is there a crossing like this near your school or home?
If not, would a crossing make it safer to cross the road?

This pedestrian crossing has traffic lights. When you press the button, a green light tells you when it is safe to cross the road.
You still need to look carefully, though.

Activities

1 Make a class map of the area around your school.
  Mark in your school. Mark in other important buildings.
  Show on your map the things that make the area safer.

2 Tell a friend about your favourite place in your local area.
  a Where is it?
  b What is it like?
  c Why do you like it?
  d What do you see there?
  What is your friend's favourite place? Why?

3 Which of these things would you like in your local area?
  Say why.
  - libraries
  - car parks
  - parks
  - shopping centres
  - swimming pool and sports centre
  Are there other things you would like in your area?

Travelling around

We make a **journey** when we travel from one place to another or go away somewhere.

Some journeys are long, some are short. How do you get from your home to school? Do you think it is a long journey?

Types of transport

Look at these pictures.
These are types of **transport**.
Have you made a journey using any of these?

Put them in order from fastest to slowest.

How many people can each one carry?
Put them in order from most people to fewest.

Where can you catch

- a bus?

- a train?

- an aeroplane?

Why do we use different types of transport?
Bicycles are not dirty or noisy.
Riding a bicycle can keep us fit.
Buses carry lots of people.
Aeroplanes travel long distances quickly.

Why do we use the other types of transport shown in the pictures?

Activities

1 Think about the journeys you make every week.
   a How long are the journeys you make?
   b What kinds of transport do you use?

2 Make a class display about the journeys made by birds and other animals. These journeys are called migrations. Use books in the library or the Internet at school to help you. Follow an animal journey on a world map.

3 Carry out a survey of the people in your class.
   a Ask each person what is their favourite way of travelling on a long journey.
   b Make a block graph of your results.
   c Which way of travelling do most people like best?

It's my world

When you make a journey, you have to choose how to travel. Then you may have to buy tickets.

If you travel to another **country**, you need a **passport**.

A trip to France

Last year, David and his family went on a long journey from Wales to Paris.

Paris is a large **city**.

It is the **capital** of France. People in France speak French. Do you know any French words? In France, you have to pay for things in Euros.

Many people in Paris travel on Metro trains. These run underground in the city centre.

This Eurostar train has arrived in Paris. On its journey it travels through the Channel Tunnel. This long tunnel goes underneath the sea from England to France.

The train journey

David went by train from Cardiff to London.

There he caught another large train.

About three hours after it had left London, the train arrived in Paris.

From the station, it was only a short taxi ride to the hotel.

Later, David went on a boat to the Eiffel Tower.

The Eiffel Tower is by the River Seine in Paris.

Activities

1 Use an atlas and follow the route that David took from Cardiff to Paris.
   a Draw a map of the route he took. Label the places he might have passed through.
   b In which other ways could David travel to Paris?

2 Collect postcards of different places. Make a class display around a map of the world. Match each postcard to the correct place on the map.

3 Ask a friend about his or her favourite kind of journey. Use these words in your questions:
   Why? When? Where to? How far?
   Record the answers on a tape for the class to listen to.

Going on holiday

People sometimes travel to other countries that are far away.
They usually make the journey in an aeroplane.

At the airport

Inside the airport, people's tickets and passports are checked.
Their cases are weighed and put on the aeroplane.

When everyone is on the aeroplane, it can take off.

Lisbon has many old buildings.

Journey to Portugal

Shakina lives in Glasgow, in Scotland.
She is going on holiday to Portugal.
The aeroplane journey lasts about four hours.

The aeroplane lands at Lisbon airport.
Lisbon is a large city.
It is the capital of Portugal.

In Portugal

In Lisbon it is hot. The Sun is shining in a clear blue sky. Shakina travels by coach to a small **town** called Cascais. The town is by the sea. There is a sandy beach.

How many boats can you see in Cascais **harbour**?

Activities

1 Use an atlas to find the places Shakina visited on her holiday.
   a Which route do you think the aeroplane took?
   b What countries did it fly over?
   c What mountains and seas did it fly over?

2 Imagine you are on holiday. Make a postcard to send home.
   a Draw the picture on the front of your postcard.
   b On the back describe
      ● what the weather is like
      ● what you have done on holiday.

3 Work in a group. Act out all the stages of going on holiday to another country.
   ● First, book your holiday with a travel agent, and then pack.
   ● Next, check in at the airport or station, and travel.
   ● Then have your holiday.
   ● Last, tell your friends about it.

Islands

These islands are part of The Bahamas.

An **island** is a piece of land with water all around it.
Do you know the names of any islands?
Most islands are separated from the **mainland** by the sea.
There are also small islands in some **lakes** and rivers.

Large and small islands

Look at the **map** of the world on page 61. How many islands can you find?
The British Isles are made up of two large islands and about a thousand smaller islands.
The world's largest island is Greenland.

The sea is cutting off a piece of the land to make a new island.

St Michael's Mount, off the coast of Cornwall, is an island only at high **tide**. At low tide you can walk to it.

Near islands

Some islands were once joined to the mainland.
The Isle of Wight was once joined to England. Thousands of years ago, it was cut off by the sea.

Distant islands

Some islands lie far out to sea. The Hawaiian Islands are the tops of high **mountains** that rise up from the bottom of the sea. **Coral** islands are made up of the shells of tiny sea animals.

Activities

1 Look at a world map or globe. Find as many islands as you can. Choose one of the islands. Write sentences saying where it is and what it is like. Use reference books or the Internet to help you. Share your work with your class.

2 Make a class collection of stamps which come from islands. Display your stamps on a wallchart.

3 a Island people often earn a living by fishing. Why is this?
  b Work in a group to make a big picture of a fishing boat. Show the nets and the fish that have been caught.

The island of Mull

Find Scotland on the map of the British Isles on page 60. How many islands can you count off the west **coast** of Scotland?
Mull is the third largest island.

Mountains and beaches

The highest mountain on Mull is called Ben More. It is 966 metres high. Mull has many beautiful **beaches**.

Tobermory has a **harbour** where fishing boats are sheltered from strong winds and rough seas.

Tobermory

Most of the people live in the largest **town**, Tobermory. There are hotels where visitors to the island can stay. Tobermory also has schools, shops, a fine park, a bank and a petrol station.

There are old castles on Mull for visitors to look around. This is Duart Castle. It was built in the 13th century. People have lived on Mull since Stone Age times.

Work

The main work on Mull is planting and cutting down trees. What do you think the trees are used for?
There are farms called crofts. Sheep and cattle are kept on some farms.
Fishing is also important.

Tourism

More than 600 000 visitors go to Mull each year.
They enjoy the beautiful scenery, beaches, wildlife and the boat trip from the mainland.

Near the coast of Mull are many smaller, rocky islands. Lighthouses help to guide ships through the dangerous waters.

Activities

1 **a** Do you think Mull would be a nice place to live and work? Tell a friend why.
   b What job would you like to do there? Say why.

2 Make a postcard which shows something about life on Mull.
   a Draw a picture on the front of your postcard.
   b Write a message on the back saying what you like about Mull.

3 Make a poster advertising Mull as *the* place to visit for a holiday.

Island transport

Look at the map of Mull.
There are nearly 200 kilometres of road on Mull.
Bus services run between the main town and the **villages**.
Many people have cars.

Trains and aeroplanes

Where is the railway on the map?
Which places does it join together?

Where is the airstrip?
Small aeroplanes belonging to local people and visitors land and take off from here.

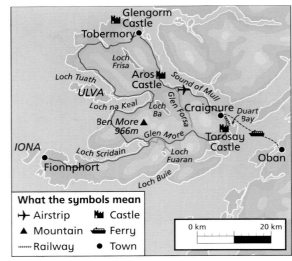

What the symbols mean
→ Airstrip   ⚑ Castle
▲ Mountain   ⛴ Ferry
⋯ Railway   ● Town

0 km   20 km

This is the only railway on Mull. Small trains take visitors to Torosay Castle..

Ferry travel

Where is the main **ferry port**?
Most passengers and goods travel to Mull on ferries from Oban on the mainland.
The **journey** takes 40 minutes.

This ferry carries passengers and **vehicles**.

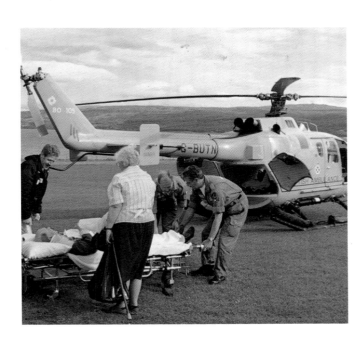

Hospital treatment

What do you think is happening in the picture?

There is a doctor on Mull but the nearest hospital is in Oban on the mainland. There is sometimes stormy **weather** when the ferries cannot sail.
Then sick or injured people have to be taken to hospital by helicopter or lifeboat.

Activities

1 Paint a picture of a view of Mull showing the sea. Add a lighthouse, a ferry, some cliffs and beaches. Add other things you might see on the island.

2 Why do people on Mull need to go to the mainland? (They might need to go to a market, a cinema or a hospital, for example.) Make a list.

3 Copy this table. Think about what you could do in summer on Mull. What could you do in winter? Write as many things as you can in the correct column.

summer	winter
swim in the sea	make a snowman

At the seaside

Have you ever been to the **seaside**?
What did it look like?
What did you do there?

Look at the pictures.
They show different seaside places.

What is the seaside?

The seaside is where the land meets
the sea.
At the edge of the sea is the **beach**.
Some beaches are made of sand.
Other beaches are made of small stones.
There are also seasides where the beach
is rocky or muddy.

What is the beach made of
in this picture?

cave

cliff

boulders   shingle

sand

sea

Why do people like visiting this seaside place? →

Seawater

Have you tasted seawater?
The water in the sea is always salty.
This salt is washed into the sea from rocks on land.

Seawater is always moving because of **waves** and **tides**.

Waves are made by the wind blowing across the water.

When the sea covers the beach, we say the tide is 'in', or it is 'high tide'. At other times, we say the tide is 'out', or it is 'low tide'.

Activities

1 Use a map or an atlas to find the seaside place nearest to your home.
   a What is it called?
   b Is it a village, a town or a city?
   c Roughly how far away from your home is it?
   d In what direction would you have to travel to reach it?
   e Try to find pictures of the seaside place. Tell a friend what it is like.

2 Look at the pictures of seasides on these two pages.
   What do you think the beach is made of in each picture?

3 With a friend, suggest a good seaside place for your class to visit. Say why you think it would be good to go there. Tell the class your ideas.

Seaside in the past

Brighton beach in 1900

People went into the sea from bathing machines at the edge of the water.

There were donkey rides and Punch and Judy shows. There were also people selling things to eat.

Look at the two photographs on this page. What do they show?

Brighton

Look at the **map** of the British Isles on page 60.
Can you find Brighton?

Once, Brighton was a fishing **village**. Then, in 1750, a doctor said that bathing in the sea there could cure diseases. Rich people went to Brighton to be cured.

Journey to Brighton

It was difficult to reach Brighton from London 250 years ago. The **journey** took about seven hours by stagecoach. The roads were bumpy and often muddy.

When the railway was built in 1841, the journey took only 100 minutes. Thousands of people could visit Brighton for the day.

Brighton today

Look at this picture of Brighton as it is today.
How is it different from Brighton 100 years ago?
Is there anything that hasn't changed?

Many people still go to Brighton for a day or for a longer holiday.

Activities

1 Find Brighton on a map or atlas. If you travelled from your home to Brighton, how would you get there? Which cities, towns or villages would you pass through or travel near? Roughly how far is Brighton from where you live?

2 Draw a picture, or make a class wall display, showing what life was like at the seaside in the past.

3 Imagine it is the summer of 1900 and you are spending a day at the seaside. Make a postcard to send to a friend. On the back, write your message. On the front, draw a picture of the seaside.

Seaside cities, towns and villages

Look at an **atlas** or a map of the world.
How many **cities** and **towns** can you find that are by the sea?
There are also many thousands of villages on or near the **coast**.

Seaside villages

Many villages were built on a hill or **cliff** near the sea. These places were easy to defend against enemies. Other villages grew up where there was good fishing.
Many villages grew into towns and cities.

Blakeney is a seaside village and small fishing port in Norfolk. People catch fish to sell to eat. Can you find Blakeney on a map of the British Isles?

The importance of rivers

Look at the picture on the left. What does it show?

Many towns and cities grew up where a river meets the sea. This is a good place to build a **port** for the large ships which carry **cargoes** from one **country** to another.

The cities of Belfast, Cardiff, Edinburgh, Dublin (left) and London in the British Isles all grew up near the mouths of rivers. Find the names of the rivers on a map of the British Isles.

Holiday resorts

Some towns grew up where people go for holidays. These are called holiday **resorts**.

This map shows some of the holiday resorts in the British Isles.
Which resort is nearest to you?

Activities

1 Carry out a survey among your friends and relatives.
Ask them
● Where is your favourite holiday resort?
● Is it a city, a town or a village?
● Why do you prefer it?
Record your findings, then show them on a class graph or chart.

2 Match the words and phrases that have the same meaning.

a	a place where ships load and unload their cargoes	1	resort
b	a big town with lots of people	2	cliff
c	a place where people go for a holiday	3	city
d	a steep wall of rock at the seaside	4	port

Seasides around the world

Nowadays people visit seasides all around the world.

Corfu

Corfu is an **island** that is part of Greece.

Corfu has sandy beaches and old buildings.

It also has many hotels, restaurants and shops.

Thousands of visitors go to Corfu on holiday in the summer when it is hot and dry.

Ferries sail from Corfu Town to the Greek **mainland**, to other Greek islands, and to Italy.

In the Florida Everglades National Park visitors can take boat rides to see alligators.

Florida

Florida is part of the United States of America.

The **weather** is warm and sunny all the year round, so people visit for holidays in every month of the year.

Florida has fine sandy beaches. It also has many places to see and things to do. These include theme parks and the Kennedy Space Center at Cape Canaveral.

Jamaica has many sandy beaches that are lined with shady trees.

Jamaica

Jamaica is an island that lies in the Caribbean Sea. The weather is warm and sunny.

Behind many of the beaches are large hotels for holidaymakers.

Every year more than a million holidaymakers visit Jamaica for the warm climate, the golden beaches and beautiful scenery.

Activities

1 Use an atlas to find Corfu, Florida and Jamaica.
   a If you were to travel to each of them from your home, how would you get there?
   b If you travelled by aeroplane, which countries, oceans and seas would you cross to reach each of them? Make a list for each place.

2 Choose one of the places – Corfu, Florida or Jamaica.
   a What can you find out about it? Use reference books or the Internet.
   b Make a little guidebook for a friend who is going there on holiday.

3 Work with some friends. Make a collection of holiday brochures. Find six seaside places in different parts of the world.

Seeing the world

How do we know what is happening all around us? Our **senses** tell us what is happening.
What are the five senses?

Our senses are working all the time.
What can you see?
What can you hear now?
How can you tell if it is raining?

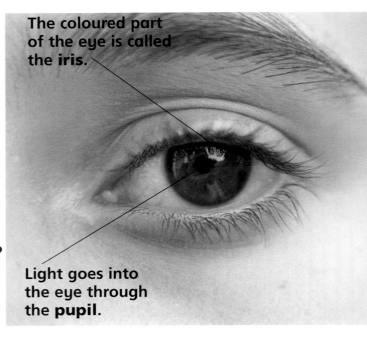

The coloured part of the eye is called the **iris**.

Light goes into the eye through the **pupil**.

Being observant

Sight is an important sense.
If you really look, you can see things you have never noticed before.
This is called being **observant**.
How observant are you?

There are 10 mistakes in this picture.
Make a list of them.

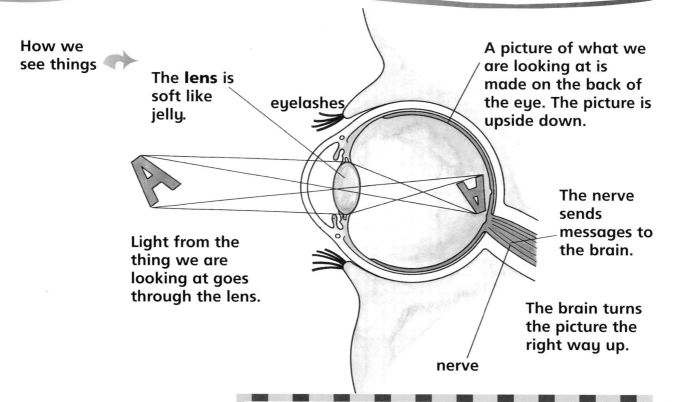

How we see things

The **lens** is soft like jelly.

eyelashes

A picture of what we are looking at is made on the back of the eye. The picture is upside down.

The nerve sends messages to the brain.

Light from the thing we are looking at goes through the lens.

The brain turns the picture the right way up.

nerve

Problems with sight

Some people cannot see all colours correctly. We say these people are 'colour blind'.

Some people cannot see at all. They may have had an accident or a disease. They may have been born with faulty eyes. We say these people are **blind**.

Activities

1 Draw and label something you can
   a see
   b hear
   c feel
   d smell
   e taste

2 How can our eyes help to keep us safe? Write down five different ways.

3 Close your eyes and say what you can see. What do you think it would be like to be blind? What things would be difficult to do?

H lping our yesight

Why do some people wear spectacles or contact lenses?
Sometimes the lenses in our eyes don't work well.
We cannot see the world around us clearly.
Then we need to use special lenses made of glass or plastic to help us see better.

Seeing small things

Some lenses help us to see very small things.
What do you use to see a minibeast clearly?

A contact lens is worn on the front of the eye. Contact lenses are usually made of soft plastic.

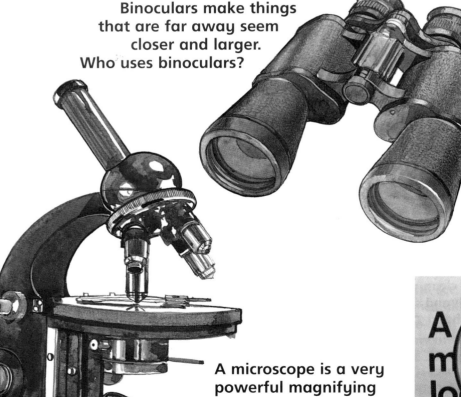

Binoculars make things that are far away seem closer and larger. Who uses binoculars?

A microscope is a very powerful magnifying glass. It lets us see things that are too small to see with only our eyes. Who uses a microscope?

A magnifying glass makes things look bigger.

A telescope also helps us to see things that are far away.

Very powerful telescopes let us see stars and **planets**. This is Jupiter seen through a telescope.

Activities

1 Make a class collection of different kinds of lenses and things with lenses in them. Look at the lenses carefully.
   a Which lenses magnify (make things look bigger)?
   b Which lenses make things look smaller?
   c Now use each of your lenses to look at a far-away object. Which is best?

2 Make a simple magnifying glass.
   ● Find a clear plastic lid, such as the lid of a coffee tin.
   ● Ask an adult to make a small hole in the middle of it with a drawing pin.
   ● Carefully cover the hole with one drop of water.
   ● Look through the water drop at writing in a newspaper or magazine. What do you see?

3 Find out about contact lenses.
   a Do you know anyone who wears contact lenses?
   b Why do they like contact lenses?
   c Is there anything they don't like about contact lenses?

Opticians at work

What is an optician?

An optician is a person who is specially trained to test your eyes.
An optician supplies contact lenses or spectacles to people who need them.

Testing our eyes

Why do we need to have our eyes tested?

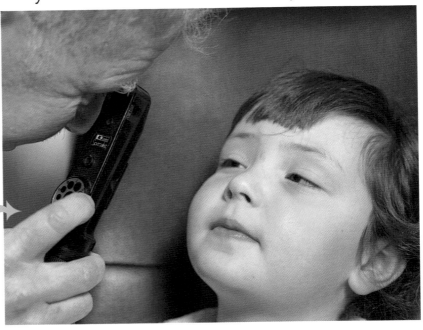

This optician is testing Maya's eyes.

First he uses a special instrument to see if there is anything wrong with the inside of the eye.

Choosing the right lenses

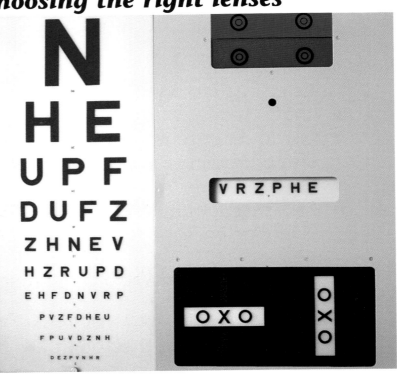

Next, the optician asks Maya to read letters from a special chart.

What do you notice about the letters on the chart?

You need good eyesight to read the letters at the bottom of the chart.

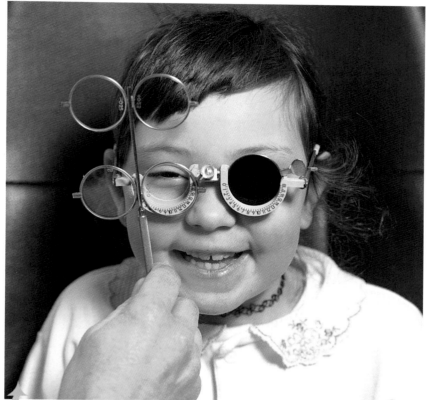

The optician tries different lenses until he finds the lenses that are best for Maya's eyes.

Recycling spectacles

Many opticians collect old spectacles that are in good condition.

The spectacles are cleaned and repaired so that they can be used again. This is called **recycling**.

The recycled spectacles are sent to other **countries** where people do not have the money to buy new spectacles.

Activities

1 Design and make your own eye-test chart.
Test your friends' eyes.

2 Ask your teacher to arrange a visit to an optician.
Or, if a friend or relative is going to see an optician,
ask if you can go too. Ask the optician if you can look at
the charts and equipment for testing people's eyes.

3 Design a poster to encourage people to save and recycle
their old spectacles.

Opticians overseas

Find Africa and Asia on the **map** of the world on page 61.

Many places in the poorer countries of Africa and Asia have no opticians.

Vision Aid Overseas

Vision Aid Overseas sends opticians to poorer countries to help to test people's eyes. They also give recycled spectacles to people who cannot afford to buy them.

In some countries of Africa and Asia, people cannot see because there are not enough opticians to discover and treat eye diseases.

On a map of Africa find these countries where Vision Aid Overseas opticians work:

- Kenya
- Uganda
- Malawi
- Tanzania
- Ghana
- Sierra Leone
- Swaziland.

Money raised by kind people helps to pay for these visits.

Why are these spectacles being sorted?

Sight Savers

People also give money to Sight Savers International to help them collect, clean, sort and recycle old spectacles.

Special motor **vehicles** carry all the equipment needed to test people's eyes and treat their eye diseases.

Sight Savers has also trained local people to do some of the optician's work.

Why is this optician from Sight Savers working in the African countryside and not in an office in a town?

Activities

1 What can you find out about some of the African countries visited by Vision Aid Overseas opticians? Collect pictures and make a class display.
   a How are the countries different?
   b How are they the same?

2 Find out more about the work of Sight Savers or Vision Aid. Use reference books or the Internet.

3 River blindness is a disease that affects many children in Africa and Asia.
   a If a blind person came into your classroom, what could you do to help him or her?
   b How do blind children read?

Recycling at home

Like old spectacles, many of the things we throw away could be reused.
They can be turned into something useful.
What is recycled at your school?
What do you recycle at home?

Glass

We go on reusing, or recycling, milk bottles until they are cracked or broken. Then the glass is melted down and made into new bottles.

Is there a bottle bank near your home?
Glass in the bottle bank is taken to a factory to be crushed, melted and made into new bottles or jars.

Empty, used milk bottles are cleaned and filled with milk again at the dairy. Then they are delivered to another customer.

Cans, paper, plastic and rags

Old metal cans can be melted down and used to make new metal objects.

Old magazines and newspapers can be used to make new paper.

Some kinds of plastic and even old rags can also be recycled.

Protecting our environment

Recycling helps to protect our **environment**. If we recycle old paper, fewer trees are cut down.

If we recycle glass, then less sand and other materials that come from the ground are needed. This means that there are fewer huge holes in the ground.

Old fruit and vegetable peelings can be put onto a **compost** heap to rot away. The compost can then be put on the soil to help more plants to grow.

Activities

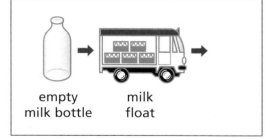

empty milk bottle   milk float

1 What happens to a milk bottle? Draw a picture or flow diagram to show what happens when we have drunk the milk.

2 Design a poster to encourage people to recycle their old bottles and other waste materials.

3 What can you use an empty plastic yoghurt pot or empty lemonade bottle for? Draw some designs and say how they can be used.

My world

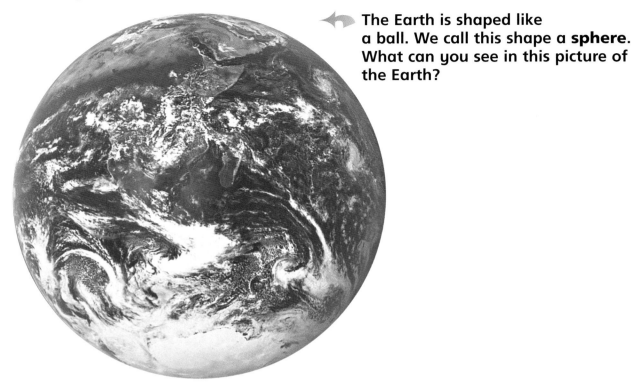

The Earth is shaped like a ball. We call this shape a **sphere**. What can you see in this picture of the Earth?

Most of the Earth is covered by sea. Only one-third is covered by land.

There are seven **continents**. What are the names of the continents? People have divided all of these continents, except for Antarctica, into **countries**. Each country has its own name and its own flag. Altogether there are about 190 countries in the world.

A globe

A **globe** is a model of the world. It shows the true shape of the land and sea. A globe can be turned, just like the Earth turns.

Can you see how the globe is tilted? Why do you think it is tilted?

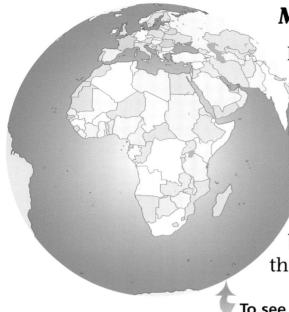

Maps

Look at a **map** of the world and a globe. Which one shows all parts of the Earth's surface at the same time?

On a globe, the world is shrunk to a very small size.

On maps, everything is also shrunk, but some maps can show every building and footpath. Who would use that sort of map?

To see Africa in more detail you need a map.

Activities

1 Choose one of the continents.

  a Lay some tracing paper over that continent on a globe. Carefully draw around the continent.

  b Now lay your tracing next to the same continent on a map of the world. How are they the same?

  c How are they different? Why are they different?

2 True or False? Copy these sentences. For each one, write 'True' if you think it is correct, or 'False' if you think it is wrong.

  a The Earth is round like a ball.

  b There is more land than sea.

  c There are seven continents.

  d All countries have the same flag.

  e A globe shows all parts of the world at the same time.

The world my larder

Food helps us to grow and stay healthy, and it gives us energy.

Where does our food come from?
Some comes from animals, some comes from plants.
Some of our food is grown in this country. Some of it comes from other countries.

Growing and buying food

Most people have to buy their food from shops, markets and supermarkets.

Many of the foods we buy in supermarkets are in cans, packets, bottles or jars.
The labels tell us what is inside. They often tell us where the food was grown or packed.

These bananas are being loaded onto a boat near to where they were picked.
The boat will take the bananas to the large ship.
The large ship takes the bananas to other countries.
Lorries then take the bananas to shops, markets and supermarkets.

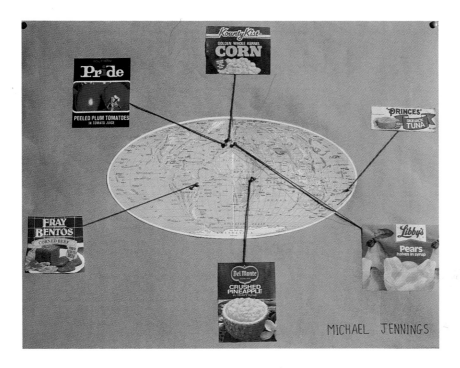

A food map

Look at this food map.
Each food label is joined to the country the food comes from.

Which of the foods would have to travel the greatest distance to reach you?

Activities

1 Make a class collection of pictures of different foods.

   Make sets of your pictures. You could have
   ● a set of foods which come from plants and a set of foods which come from animals
   ● a set of foods grown or made in this country and a set which come from other countries
   ● a set of fresh foods and a set of frozen or dried foods.

   How many more sets can you think of?

2 After a meal, draw a large picture of your plate and the foods you ate.

   Try to find out where each item was bought, grown or made. Write this on your drawing.

China

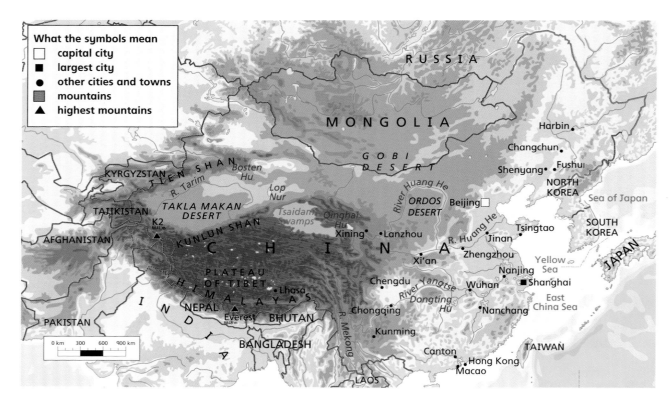

What the symbols mean
- ☐ capital city
- ■ largest city
- • other cities and towns
- ▦ mountains
- ▲ highest mountains

Find China on the map of the world on page 61.
Which two countries are larger than China?
More than 1 billion (1000 million) people live in China. That is more than in any other country.

Where people live

Look at the map of China. What can you tell about the country?
Most people live near rivers. Many of them are farmers who grow rice and other crops. Their homes often do not have electricity or running water.

Chinese cities

What is the **capital city** of China?
Which is the largest city?
In the cities, many people live in small houses or **flats** with only one or two rooms.

Very few Chinese own a car. Instead they use bicycles to get to work or school, or to the shops.

China is changing

China is still quite a poor country, although that is changing.
New schools, farms and factories are being built.
People from foreign countries are being encouraged to visit China.
Chinese people are going abroad to learn new ways to tackle China's problems.

Activities

1 Look at a map of the world. Find your nearest large city on the map. Then find Shanghai.
   a If you were to fly from your city to Shanghai, which countries might you fly over?
   b Find out something about each of these countries.
   c Which seas or mountains might you fly over?

2 a Make a class collection of pictures and small things that show what life is like in China.
   b Label each picture and thing.
   c Say what it shows about China.

3 a Write down what you think the weather would be like in Shanghai or Beijing today.
   b How can you find out if you are right?

Living in Shanghai

Look at this picture of Shanghai. How is it different from where you live?

The city of Shanghai is the biggest **port** in China and one of the largest ports in the world.

The city is built beside the Huangpu River.

There are many fine old buildings by the Huangpu River in Shanghai.

Meet Mei-Ling

Mei-Ling lives with her parents in a small flat. She is six years old. Like most children in China, Mei-Ling is an only child. She has no brothers or sisters.

A school day

For breakfast, Mei-Ling eats rice porridge with vegetables and steamed bread. Like most Chinese, Mei-Ling drinks lots of tea without milk or sugar.

Mei-Ling walks to the local primary school. School starts at seven o'clock and doesn't finish until half past four.

Lunch is usually noodles with stir-fried vegetables and perhaps a little meat or fish.

Lessons

At school, Mei-Ling's class has more than 50 children. They study Chinese, maths, music, craft, PE and science. Mei-Ling's favourite lesson is craft.

Winter in Shanghai is cold, but the school has no heating. The children have to wear warm clothes.

Activities

1 Copy this table to compare your life with that of Mei-Ling. The table has been started for you. Try to think of more things to add.

	Mei-Ling	Me
Age	6 years	
Home	Flat	
Brothers and sisters	None	
Favourite food		
School uniform		
Number of children in class		
Favourite lesson		

2 a Would you like to live in Shanghai? Say why.
 b What would you enjoy?
 c What would you dislike?

The British Isles

ATLANTIC OCEAN

SHETLAND ISLANDS

ORKNEY ISLANDS

NORTH SEA

OUTER HEBRIDES

Isle of Skye

Isle of Mull

Inverness

Aberdeen

SCOTLAND

Edinburgh

Glasgow

R. Foyle

Londonderry

NORTHERN IRELAND

Belfast

Newcastle

Isle of Man

IRISH SEA

R. Ouse

Leeds

Manchester

Liverpool

R. Shannon

REPUBLIC OF IRELAND

R. Barrow

Dublin

Limerick

Kilkenny

Cork

WALES

R. Trent

Nottingham

Norwich

R. Severn

Birmingham

R. Great Ouse

Cambridge

Ipswich

ENGLAND

Swansea

Oxford

London

Cardiff

Bristol

R. Thames

Reading

Dover

CELTIC SEA

Portsmouth

Brighton

Exeter

Isle of Wight

ATLANTIC OCEAN

ENGLISH CHANNEL

0 km   50 100 km

Guernsey

Jersey

FRANCE

The world

Arctic Ocean

Arctic Ocean

Arctic Ocean

Greenland
Denmark

ICELAND

North Atlantic Ocean

North Pacific Ocean

Alaska
US

C A N A D A

UNITED STATES

MEXICO

BAHAMAS

CUBA
JAMAICA
Caribbean Sea

COSTA RICA
ECUADOR
PERU

COLOMBIA
VENEZUELA

B R A Z I L

BOLIVIA

PARAGUAY

URUGUAY

A R G E N T I N A

CHILE

South Pacific Ocean

South Atlantic Ocean

Equator

NORWAY
SWEDEN
FINLAND
ESTONIA
LATVIA
LITHUANIA
DENMARK
UNITED KINGDOM
IRELAND
NETHER-LANDS
GERMANY
POLAND
BELARUS
UKRAINE
BELGIUM
SWITZ.
AUSTRIA
HUNGARY
CZECH REP.
SLOVAKIA
ROMANIA
BULGARIA
FRANCE
ITALY
GREECE
SPAIN
PORTUGAL

MOROCCO
ALGERIA
TUNISIA
LIBYA
EGYPT

MAURITANIA
SENEGAL
GUINEA
SIERRA LEONE
IVORY COAST
GHANA
MALI
NIGER
NIGERIA
CAMEROON
CHAD
SUDAN
CONGO
GABON
DEMOCRATIC REPUBLIC OF CONGO
ANGOLA
NAMIBIA
BOTSWANA
ZAMBIA
ZIMBABWE
SOUTH AFRICA
MOZAMBIQUE
TANZANIA
KENYA
ETHIOPIA
SOMALIA
MADAGASCAR

TURKEY
SYRIA
ISRAEL
JORDAN
IRAQ
IRAN
SAUDI ARABIA
YEMEN
OMAN

R U S S I A

KAZAKHSTAN
UZBEKISTAN
TURKMENISTAN
AFGHANISTAN
PAKISTAN

MONGOLIA

C H I N A

NORTH KOREA
SOUTH KOREA
JAPAN
TAIWAN

NEPAL
BHUTAN
BANGLADESH
INDIA

SRI LANKA

Indian Ocean

VIETNAM
LAOS
THAILAND

PHILIPPINES

MALAYSIA

I N D O N E S I A

PAPUA NEW GUINEA

AUSTRALIA

NEW ZEALAND

North Pacific Ocean

South Pacific Ocean

Equator

A N T A R C T I C A

Where is it?

The children in the picture on the cover of this book live in Thailand. Look in an atlas, in reference books, or on the Internet to find out where Thailand is. Is it near the sea? What is the capital city?

Africa	
America	
Asia	
Europe	
Oceania	

0 km 1000 2000 3000 km

see also: **The Oxford Infant Atlas**

Glossary

Atlas A book of maps.

Beach The strip of sand, shingle, mud or rock where a sea or lake meets the land.

Blind Being unable to see.

Bungalow A house with no upstairs rooms.

Bypass A road that goes around a city, town or village.

Capital The most important city in a country.

Cargo Goods carried by lorries, aeroplanes and ships.

City A large and important town. A city usually has a cathedral or a university.

Cliff A steep wall of rock, especially on the coast.

Coast The seashore and the land close to it.

Compost Plant food made from rotting leaves, vegetable peelings, etc.

Continent One of the seven big pieces of land on the Earth.

Coral A hard substance made from the shells of tiny sea animals.

Country A land with its own name, government, flag and postage stamps. Most countries have their own money.

Environment Your surroundings.

Ferry A ship used for carrying people or things across a river or narrow sea.

Flat A set of rooms for living in, usually on one floor of a building.

Globe A ball or sphere with a map of the whole world on it.

Harbour A place where ships can shelter or unload.

Iris The coloured part of the eye around the pupil.

Island A piece of land surrounded by water.

Job The work that someone does, often to earn money.

Journey Going from one place to another.

Lake A large area of water surrounded by land.

Lens (1) Part of the eye. (2) A curved piece of glass or plastic used to make things larger or smaller.

Mainland The main part of a country, not the islands around it.

Map A drawing of part or all of the Earth's surface as if you were looking down on it.

Mountain A very high hill.

Observant To be observant is to look carefully at everything around you.

Optician Someone who tests your eyesight and supplies spectacles.

Passport An official document that you must have if you wish to travel to other countries.

Pavement A raised path at the side of the road that separates people from cars and other traffic.

Pedestrian Someone who is walking.

Plan A drawing showing what something looks like from above, or a map of a town or district.

Planet One of the large objects that travel around the Sun.

Port A harbour, or a town or city with a harbour.

Pupil The small hole in the centre of the eye.

Recycle To treat waste material so that it can be used again.

Reflect To make light bounce off something.

Resort A place where people go for their holidays.

Seaside A place, such as a village, town or city, by the sea.

Sense The ability to see, hear, touch, taste or smell.

Sphere Shaped like a ball.

Street A road in a city or town.

Street furniture The lights, seats, litter bins, post boxes, telephone boxes, signs and other objects on roads, streets and pavements.

Tide The rising and falling of the level of the sea, which happens twice a day.

Town A place that is larger than a village and smaller than a city.

Traffic Cars, buses, lorries, bicycles, etc. travelling along a road.

Transport (1) Moving people, animals or things from one place to another. (2) Motor vehicles and aeroplanes.

Vehicle Something which transports people, animals or things.

Village A group of houses and other buildings in the country.

Wave A moving ridge of water on the sea, formed by the wind blowing over the water.

Weather The rain, wind, snow, sunshine, etc. at a particular time or place.

Index